My Pet Hamster
& Gerbils

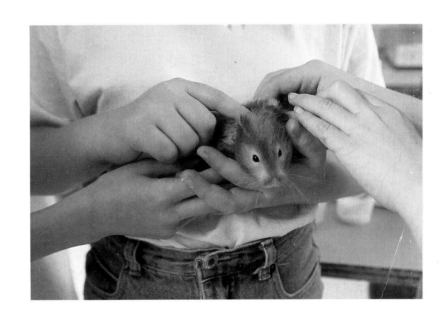

My Pet Hamster

& Gerbils

by **LeeAnne Engfer**
photographs by **Andy King**

Lerner Publications Company • Minneapolis

To Martha Brennecke—L.E.

Acknowledgments

Thanks to Raymond Yu and his fourth grade class: Ana Albrecht, Ben Brody, Nellie Connolly, Kate Cowley, Jacob Harstad, Kara Johnson, Peter Landwehr, Melissa Lee, Laura Markee, Kira Moscowitz, Spencer Nelson, Nick Olson, Katie Piirainen, David Ramsay, Alex Schned, Maggie Severns-O'Neill, Colin Snover, Tiffany Spoor, Jason Stubbings, Lauren Taylor, and Alexa Weingarden, with special thanks to David and Melissa.

The publisher would like to thank Dr. Barbara Leppke for her assistance with this book.

Photos on pp. 10, 40, & 52 (both) by Michael Gilroy, reproduced by permission of Aquila Photographics; pp. 25 & 56 by Jim Simondet, Independent Picture Service.

Library of Congress Cataloging-in-Publication Data

Engfer, LeeAnne, 1963–
    My pet hamster and gerbils / by LeeAnne Engfer ; photographs by Andy King.
        p.   cm. — (All about pets)
    Includes bibliographical references and index.
    Summary: Provides useful information about the habits of hamsters and gerbils and how to care for them as pets.
    ISBN 0–8225–2261–6 (hardcover)
    ISBN 0–8225–9794–2 (paperback)
    1. Hamsters as pets—Juvenile literature. 2. Gerbils as pets—Juvenile literature. [1. Hamsters. 2. Gerbils.] I. King, Andy, ill. II. Title. III. Series
    SF459.H3E54   1997
    636.9'356—dc21   96–37908

Manufactured in the United States of America
1 2 3 4 5 6 — JR — 02 01 00 99 98 97

Contents

CHAPTER 1

A hamster goes to school...

Normally you don't think of hamsters as being very dangerous. I mean, can you imagine a horror movie about a big, vicious hamster? I don't think so. Hamsters are cute and small and cuddly, like teddy bears. But I have a story about a girl in my class who was bitten by a snake. And it was all my hamster's fault!

My name is David. I'm in fourth grade at the Blake School, near Minneapolis, Minnesota. During the school year, my pet hamster, Lightning, lives in our classroom. Lightning is really Lightning II. I named her after a hamster in another class at school. The original Lightning is black and white. My hamster is brown and white.

This is our class pet, my hamster, Lightning II.

I got my hamster two years ago. My friend Jason and I gave each other a hamster for our birthdays. Our birthdays are only 29 days apart. I brought my hamster to school once, and the other kids liked her. I decided to leave her there, since my mom kind of hated having Lightning in the house.

Lots of kids in my class have hamsters or gerbils for pets. Maggie has a hamster named Elsie. Elsie is black and white like a cow. Maggie says that hamsters surprise you. They're tiny, but they can run fast and jump.

It's great having Lightning in our class. Hamsters are fun to watch. When you put them on the floor, they run really fast. Kate likes hamsters because they're cute and small. Tiffany likes how their whiskers twitch. And Ana likes their soft fur.

Melissa has pet gerbils at home. She knows a lot about hamsters, too.

All the kids in my class like Lightning and help take care of her.

Hamsters and gerbils make good pets because they don't cost very much. Their food and bedding are not very expensive. They are clean, and they don't take up much space. They're also easy to take care of. I have a dog at home, so I know dogs are more work. Dogs have to be walked, and they need a lot of attention. But hamsters and gerbils are simpler. You just have to feed them, clean the cage, and play with them.

Types of Hamsters

Most pet hamsters are golden hamsters. The name comes from the color of the fur, reddish brown or gold. They are also sometimes called Syrian hamsters. Other kinds of hamsters are the dwarf or Russian hamster, the Chinese hamster, the Siberian, and the common hamster.

The dwarf hamster is smaller than the golden hamster. Dwarf hamsters are only two to three inches long. The Chinese hamster is about the size of a mouse. The Siberian hamster comes from the north of Asia. Its fur turns white in winter. Then there's the common hamster, the biggest one. It can grow as large as a rat. Common hamsters are wild, and they live in Europe. They are not pets, they're pests.

Hamsters come in many colors. Besides golden or reddish brown, hamsters can be cinnamon (light orange), tortoiseshell (a mixture of black, orange or brown, and white), gray, black, or white. They can have either short or long hair. Most hamsters have a white or cream-colored belly.

Our teacher, Mr. Yu, says that we can learn about responsibility by having a pet. Mr. Yu wants us to be respectful of animals and to treat them well. We've learned one thing—if you don't treat a hamster with respect, it will pee on you! If your hamster pees on you, that means it's mad or afraid.

Mr. Yu taught us how to hold Lightning and keep her calm.

Books can tell you a lot about animals. We all wrote reports on hamsters when Lightning joined our class.

Hamsters and gerbils are rodents. Some other kinds of rodents are guinea pigs, mice, rats, squirrels, porcupines, and gophers. Rodents have teeth that *never* stop growing. That's why hamsters and gerbils are always gnawing and chewing on whatever they can find. They need to grind down their teeth. If they don't, their teeth will keep growing until they poke right out of their heads! When Lightning yawns, her teeth look really big.

Hamsters are three to six inches long, about the size of my hand. They have a stubby little tail. Both hamsters and gerbils have bright black eyes. Their eyes make them look very curious and alert. But hamsters can't see very well—they're nearsighted.

One thing I really like about my hamster is her tiny front paws. A hamster's paws look like little hands. Lightning uses her paws like hands, too. She holds her food up to her mouth to chew it. Gerbils also have little paws.

Hamsters and gerbils sometimes stand on their back legs. Gerbils can make a loud thumping noise with their back legs. In the wild, gerbils thump to keep other animals from attacking.

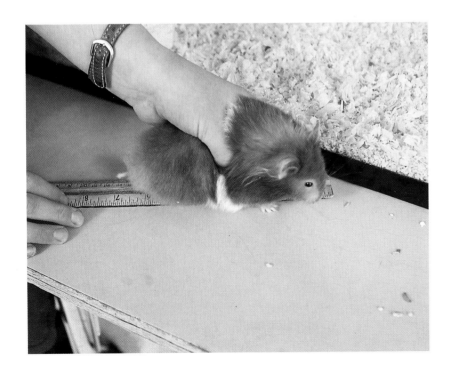

Lightning is about six inches long, not including her tail.

Hamsters are usually friendly. If you don't scare them or bother them, they don't bite. Mr. Yu says that Lightning has a "calming effect" on our class. I don't know about that. I remember one time when she definitely did not calm anyone down.

We have another pet in our class, too. It's a corn snake. Have you ever seen one? They are really pretty. They're coral colored, a light red. Anyway, one day in class Kate was holding the hamster. Someone else was standing nearby holding the snake. All of a sudden, the snake extended itself to its full length, toward Lightning. The snake looked like it was going to eat her! Kate got scared and dropped the hamster. The snake bit her finger.

Ruby, our snake, is pretty small—we don't know if she could eat a hamster. We keep Ruby and Lightning apart, just in case.

Lightning looks
innocent, but she has a
mischievous side, too.

Mr. Yu said he couldn't believe how cool Kate
was about it, even though her finger was bleeding.

Hamsters bite sometimes, too. Most of the time it
doesn't hurt. It just feels like a light pinch. But if
they're scared or acting bad, they might bite hard.
That hurts.

Hamsters eat almost anything...

An aquarium doesn't seem much like a desert, where wild hamsters live. Lightning seems happy in her cage, though.

Lightning's cage is an aquarium. Aquariums make good cages for hamsters and gerbils because they can't chew through glass. The aquarium should be at least a 10-gallon tank. That way your pet has plenty of room to move around and get exercise. In a smaller aquarium, there may not be enough room for the air to move around. Warm, humid air can make a hamster sick. Hamsters come from the desert, where it's very dry. In general, the bigger the cage is, the happier your pet will be.

You can also buy cages made of metal, wood, or plastic. Hamsters and gerbils can chew through metal and plastic, so these are not as good. If you get a metal cage, be sure the bars are close together. If the bars are more than half an inch apart, a hamster or gerbil can squeeze through them and escape.

Glass walls are safest— and they give your hamster a good view.

Pets also can escape from the top of a cage. It's important to keep the top of your hamster's aquarium covered and weighted down. Once I forgot to put the weights on top of the cage, and that night Lightning got out. You also want to keep other animals (if you have them) from getting to your hamster. Cats would love to eat a hamster or gerbil for dinner!

Actually, that did happen to a hamster that used to be in another class at school. A kid took the hamster home for the weekend, and his cat killed it! He told the teacher that the hamster got lost. But he told his friend what really happened, and the friend told everyone else at school.

We cover Lightning's cage with wire mesh, weighted down with hockey pucks.

Pets depend on you for everything. It's up to you to give your hamster fresh food and water every day.

We keep Lightning's cage on a shelf in the back of our classroom. The shelf is away from the windows. You should never put the cage in direct sunlight. That's really bad for hamsters. If they get too hot, they can die.

At the side of the cage there's a water bottle. Hamsters and gerbils need fresh water every day. The water bottles that hang inside the cage work the best. When the animal is thirsty, it just goes up to the nozzle and takes a drink.

Lightning makes a nest in the corner of the cage. That's where she sleeps. Some people put a nesting house or box in the cage. In the wild, hamsters dig tunnels into the dirt or sand.

Someone has to watch Lightning while her cage is being cleaned.

Kids in our class chip in to buy Lightning's bedding and food. Nick and I take turns cleaning the cage. Most of the time, Lightning pees and poops in the same corner of the cage—it's her bathroom. Every day one of us cleans out that corner with a spoon. We also take turns changing all the bedding once a week. If you don't clean the cage, the hamster starts to smell like the cage.

Once a month or so, Nick and I wash everything in the cage with warm, soapy water. We also wash out the water bottle.

The cage has to have plenty of bedding on the bottom. We use wood shavings (pine or cedar). You can also use tissue like Kleenex, wood chips, sawdust, cat litter, dried corncob pellets, hay, straw, or cloth. I've read that hay is most like what hamsters have in the wild.

Cleaning the cage is really pretty easy. Of course, I have friends to help.

Hamsters do not get along with other hamsters. You should not keep two hamsters in one cage, unless you want them to mate. Even brother and sister hamsters end up fighting. There is one way to let two hamsters live together. Hamsters that are neutered or spayed ("fixed" so they can't have babies) can get along together. I don't know anyone who actually had the operation done on a hamster. But my vet told me lots of people bring hamsters in for neutering and spaying.

Unlike hamsters, gerbils get along together, even if they are not fixed. Most people who have gerbils keep a pair of them. But if you don't have them fixed, you should get either two females or two males. Otherwise, you will end up with a hundred gerbils. It's best to buy a pair that has been raised together.

Lightning is a female. When hamsters are young, it's harder to tell females from males.

You can't say hamsters have good table manners. It's a hamster's instinct to put food everywhere.

There's a food dish in the cage, but Lightning usually makes a big mess of her food. She gets it everywhere. She likes to hide it, too. We buy hamster food that's a mixture of seeds and grains. We also give her fresh food, like lettuce, carrots, apples, and pears. I like to make her a little salad, like a Caesar salad without the dressing.

If she's hungry, Lightning eats just about anything we give her. So we only give her food that's healthy.

In the wild, hamsters are omnivorous. That means they eat anything. They eat greens and lots of seeds. They also love insects. I wonder how Lightning would like it if I gave her a cricket?

Alexa gives her hamster pickle relish and turkey. Kate says her hamster's favorite foods are sunflower seeds and pumpkin seeds. I think every hamster loves sunflower seeds. In fact, hamsters like them almost *too* much. Sometimes they won't eat anything else, and they get sick.

What to Feed a Hamster or Gerbil

- commercial hamster food or pellets

- nuts—peanuts, filberts, walnuts (unsalted)
- cereal grains, such as wheat, oats, and corn
- sunflower seeds (only as a special treat)
- pumpkin seeds
- rolled oats

- dandelion greens
- alfalfa
- clover
- meadow grass
- sow thistle

- fruits of all kinds

- carrots
- cauliflower
- potatoes (no leaves or sprouting eyes)

- tomatoes
- spinach
- celery
- cucumbers
- lettuce
- chicory

- meat
- cottage cheese
- yogurt

- twigs or branches from beech trees, maples, willows, or fruit trees

- dog biscuits

Some foods are poisonous to hamsters and gerbils. Do not feed your pet any of the following foods:
raw beans; sprouting potatoes; the green part of potatoes and tomatoes; canned or frozen vegetables.

After we give Lightning fresh food, Mr. Yu makes sure we take away anything she doesn't eat right away. Otherwise, Lightning might hide it and it would go bad. If she eats rotten food, she will get sick.

Pets are not all that different from people. They like to eat a variety of foods. I try to give Lightning a varied diet. I don't want her to get bored.

I like to watch Lightning eat. She picks up her food with her hands.

CHAPTER 3

She climbed to the top of the wheel and escaped...

I wonder what it's like to have 20 kids pick you up all the time! Lightning puts up with a lot.

Hamsters like to sleep during the day. Anyone who has one knows that hamsters become active at night. That's because, in the desert, where wild hamsters live, it's better to look for food at night. It's safer and cooler at night than in the daytime.

Poor Lightning—her natural routine is sort of topsy-turvy. She tries to sleep all day. But living in the classroom with all of us, she can't sleep as much as she wants. We take her out to play sometimes. When I keep her at home, I let her sleep during the day. I play with her in the late afternoon or early evening.

With the plastic ball, Lightning can be outside her cage, but she won't get lost.

Playing with a hamster is one of the best parts about having one. Lightning likes to run around outside the cage at least once a day. I don't blame her—who would want to stay in a cage all day?

At school, we let Lightning run inside one of those clear plastic balls. It's funny to watch her, because she's always crashing into things. Most of the time she bumps into walls.

I don't take Lightning outside very often. Hamsters can't handle direct sunlight for very long. They might fry! Melissa doesn't take her gerbils outside at all. She's afraid they might decide to escape.

One time, Maggie took her hamster outside and put her on the grass. For a long time, Elsie didn't move. Then she lay down next to a twig about the size of a pencil. Maggie thinks Elsie was trying to hide behind it—as if Maggie couldn't see her!

We let Lightning run on a table, too. We watch her so she doesn't fall off.

Lightning runs in her wheel a lot. She'll run for a long time, like she's in a marathon.

I haven't bought very many toys for Lightning. I give her the cardboard rolls from toilet paper and paper towels. She likes to crawl through them. And she has her exercise wheel—that's her favorite toy. I've heard that hamsters can get addicted to running in the wheel. They can't stop.

Sometimes I give Lightning a twig or a wooden clothespin to chew on. I give her a stick with rough bark, and I make sure it's clean. I also get chew circles made of wood at the pet store.

When I pick up Lightning, I cup my hand around her. Sometimes I pick her up with two hands, one underneath her and one above her. I try not to squeeze her too hard. Melissa doesn't hold her gerbils too tightly either. It works best if you let them have a little room to move. But you need to have a firm enough hold that they can't jump out of your hands. Do not pick up a gerbil by the tail. You could actually pull the tail off.

I don't like to wake Lightning up when she's asleep. But if I do, here's how I do it. First I say her name very softly. I touch her fur lightly. When she wakes up, she starts to yawn and stretch. I give her a couple of pumpkin seeds and talk to her. Then, when she's pretty much awake, I pick her up.

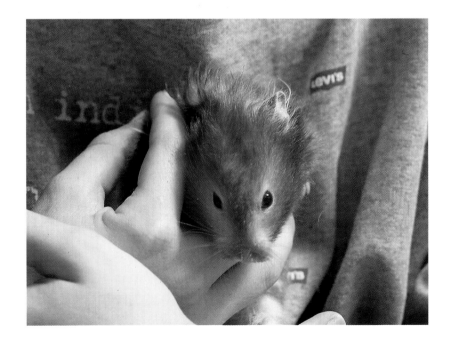

Lightning likes me to hold her, but only when she's in the mood.

Dangers to Hamsters & Gerbils

Most of the dangerous situations hamsters and gerbils are likely to encounter happen **outside the cage.** So it is very important to **supervise your hamster or gerbil when you let it play or run outside its cage.**

- Do not play with your pet on a **table** unless you watch it closely. Your pet could **fall** and be hurt.
- Make sure your pet doesn't escape under a **door** or get caught in a closing door.
- Be careful not to **step** or **sit on** your hamster or gerbil!
- Don't leave **small, pointed objects** such as needles or nails in an area where you let your pet play.
- Do not let your pet eat **houseplants,** since they could be poisonous.

- Keep your hamster or gerbil away from **hot items** such as the stove.
- Keep any **electric wires** hidden so your pet is not tempted to chew on them.
- Do not allow other pets to come into the room when your hamster or gerbil is out of its cage. Cats have been known to kill or injure hamsters and gerbils.
- **Wood stains or varnishes** can make your pets sick, so don't let them chew on furniture. (Your parents will appreciate that, too.)

Inside the cage, there are other risks:

- If you have a **cage** with **bars,** make sure the bars are not more than ½ inch (1.3 cm) apart. If they are farther apart, your pet could squeeze through them and escape.
- If a **metal cage** gets **rusty,** your pet could be poisoned from chewing on the bars.

- Never put a hamster's or gerbil's cage in **direct sunlight** or over a **heating vent.** These can cause heat stroke.
- A **metal running wheel** with bars that are too far apart can be dangerous. Tails and feet can get caught between the bars.

It will probably happen one time or another—your hamster or gerbil will escape. At least it's happened to everyone I know. Kara's hamster was lost for two weeks. Then one day she just showed up in the living room. Peter's hamster disappeared, and they found it in his mom's closet.

The night I forgot to put the hockey pucks on top of the cage, Lightning got out. She climbed to the top of the wheel and escaped. The next morning, we couldn't find her. But we came up with a plan to get her back. We put the cage on the floor and stacked books next to the cage like steps. We put a trail of food on the books.

Lightning ate her way to the top of the steps . . .

. . . and she found her
way back home.

Our plan worked. When we weren't looking, Lightning came out from her hiding place. She followed the trail of food all the way up the steps. When she reached the top, we gently pushed her into the cage.

I tamed her in a few days...

At the end of the school year, I took Lightning back home with me. I keep her in my room or in the basement. When she's in my room, I can hear her running on her wheel at night. The squeaking wakes me up sometimes. But usually I can sleep through it.

Jason and I got our hamsters two years ago at a pet store in our neighborhood. Most of my friends bought their hamsters and gerbils at pet stores. I think Kate got her hamster from someone who was breeding them.

Lightning is a good roommate, but sometimes she's kind of loud.

Hamsters don't need much equipment to be healthy and happy.

The week before we got Lightning, my mom and I went to the store and bought all the supplies. We bought an aquarium, an exercise wheel, a ceramic food dish, a water bottle, bedding, food, and the exercise ball. We spent about $40 for everything, including the hamster. If you are planning to buy a hamster or gerbil, you can expect to spend $30 to $50 right away for supplies. After that, the cost of food and litter is cheap. It's probably no more than $10 a month.

Before we picked out a hamster, we got the cage ready for her. We washed all the supplies with soap and water. Then we put bedding in the cage.

When we bought Lightning, she was about five weeks old. Most books say to buy a hamster or gerbil when it is four to seven weeks old. It will be ready to leave its mother, but you will still be able to tame it. Older hamsters and gerbils are harder to tame.

We went to the store in the evening, when the hamsters are most active. They had about 10 baby hamsters. They were only a couple of inches long, pinkie size. They were all piled in a corner, sleeping on top of each other. I picked out Lightning because she was soft and cute. She seemed to be healthy. She looked clean and dry, and her fur was shiny. Her eyes were bright.

Lightning hasn't changed a lot since she was a baby. She's bigger, of course.

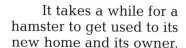
It takes a while for a hamster to get used to its new home and its owner.

We brought Lightning home in a box. We put some litter from the pet store cage into the box. That way she would feel at home. When we got to our house, we put the old litter in her new cage. She went to a corner and burrowed.

At first Lightning did not like to be touched. She would run from my hand when I tried to touch her. But then my babysitter helped me tame her. Every day, we went to Lightning's cage. First we talked softly to her. Then I put a sunflower seed in my hand and put my hand in Lightning's cage. After a few days, Lightning took the seed from my hand.

After Lightning began eating from my hand, I started to pick her up. Every day for a week, I held her. By the end of the week, she was used to being held. I could take her out and play with her.

I try to play with Lightning once a day. I let her run loose in my bedroom. But I have to make sure to keep the door shut. Otherwise Scooter, my dog, would go crazy and chase Lightning. Scooter barks at the cage a lot.

Scooter loves to watch Lightning in her cage. It's really funny.

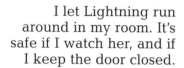

I let Lightning run around in my room. It's safe if I watch her, and if I keep the door closed.

Hamsters lead a pretty simple life. They spend a lot of their time grooming themselves. They lick their fur and use their tiny paws to wash their face. They keep their fur nice and clean. They like to eat and they like to take naps. They also love to climb. Lightning tries to get out of the cage by climbing up the side with the water bottle.

Hamsters like a change in routine sometimes. They get bored if nothing ever changes. That's why I let Lightning out pretty often. I give her a cardboard tube from a roll of paper towels to play with. Sometimes I put a branch or some dry grass in her cage. I pet her, too.

Fun Facts about Hamsters

- The word *hamster* comes from the German word *hamstern,* which means to store or hoard.

- The entire world population of pet hamsters originated from one mother and her litter, discovered in 1930 in Syria. Hamsters arrived in the United States in 1938.

- A hamster's heart beats 375 to 400 beats per minute, and it averages 75 breaths a minute!

- Baby hamsters are called pups or kittens.

- Hamsters carry their babies in their pouches. Hamsters also use their pouches to defend themselves. They puff out their pouches if they see an enemy approaching, so they look bigger. Gerbils don't have pouches.

Give your pet hamster tunnels to run through. Your hamster will feel like a wild hamster burrowing in the ground.

A hamster's main activities are napping and sleeping, gnawing and nibbling, and running and climbing. They also hoard food and burrow. That is how hamsters behave in the wild.

In the deserts where wild hamsters live, hamsters burrow deep into the earth. They make tunnels. I have a plastic tube that is like a tunnel. Lightning loves to run through it. Pet stores sell cages with a lot of those plastic tubes linked together. I bet hamsters love them.

In the wild, hamsters save up piles of food, because food is hard to find. Even a tame hamster like Lightning hoards food.

Hamsters can stuff a lot of food into their pouches. Their pouches are huge. They stretch from the inside of the lips all the way down to their shoulders. With its pouches full, a hamster's head is double its normal size. Sometimes Lightning fills her pouches with food. A little bit later, she strokes her paws along the sides of the pouches to push the food out. I like to watch her do that.

Hamsters communicate mainly by scent. They send messages by giving out scents. The scents come from special glands on the sides of their body. Hamsters also mark their territory that way. Gerbils also have a scent gland, on their belly.

Lightning hides food around the cage. I have to make sure she doesn't hide fresh food.

A hamster knows its owner by his or her smell. Hamsters also can tell their owner's voice from other people's. They don't like high-pitched or squealing noises, so don't scream at your hamster.

Hamsters and gerbils are quiet. They normally don't squeal or squeak unless they're afraid.

I'm pretty sure Lightning knows I'm her best friend.

Lightning is happy when we play together.

Lightning doesn't really have a lot of moods, but I try to guess why she does what she does. When a hamster's ears point back, that means it's in a bad mood or afraid. When it sits up on its back legs, it's on the alert for danger, or ready to fight. When it creeps along close to the ground, that means it may be nervous. When a hamster leaps into the air, it's a leap of joy. That animal is feeling good.

CHAPTER 5

Gerbils will run all over you...

Melissa gives
Frisky a kiss.

My friend Melissa has three gerbils. She used to have two, Frisky and Missy, but Missy died. Then Melissa's family decided to get two more gerbils.

At the pet store, the gerbils were named Bert and Ernie. When Melissa brought them home, she gave them new names. The light one is called Flower Rose, and the darker one is Sourpuss. I guess he's not as friendly. She calls them "my funky dudes."

Frisky is very dark brown—almost black. I think she's really cool looking. I'd like to have a black gerbil. Most gerbils are light brown or reddish brown, with a few black hairs. Underneath the outer coat, they have a layer of gray fur. Their belly fur is lighter—white or cream. Gerbils are smaller than hamsters. Most gerbils are only about three or four inches long.

Gerbils look sort of like mice. I like their long tails.

Melissa uses pine or cedar shavings in her cages, just like I do. She uses water bottles like my hamster's, too.

Melissa keeps her gerbils in an aquarium. Frisky has her own aquarium, and Flower Rose and Sourpuss live in another one. Their cages are underneath the television in the living room. I guess if the TV show Melissa is watching gets too boring, she can always watch the gerbils.

Taking care of gerbils is a lot like taking care of hamsters. Melissa has to feed her gerbils and give them fresh water every day. She changes the bedding once a week. Gerbils also need a nesting house to sleep in. You put it inside the cage. The nesting house can be a plastic house that you buy at a pet store. Or you can use a wood or tin box with a door.

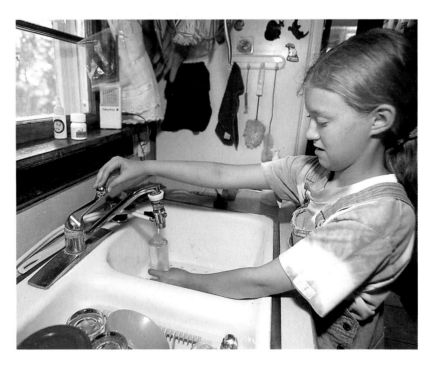

Melissa buys gerbil food at the pet store. It's not that different from hamster food. Melissa also feeds the gerbils fresh food—lettuce, carrots, crackers, apples, and avocado. She says they like all kinds of foods. In the spring, she gave Frisky a dandelion to eat.

The gerbils also have an exercise wheel. I have heard that a gerbil can get its tail caught in a metal wheel if the wheel is the wrong size. The tail could be cut off. It's probably a good idea to buy a solid plastic wheel, with no rungs. But Melissa hasn't had any problems with her metal wheel so far.

Melissa and her friend Ana feed the gerbils some seeds.

Gerbils are really active. When you take them out of their cages, they want to run!

Melissa also has a plastic ball for the gerbils to run in. Sourpuss and Flower Rose don't have the hang of it yet. They're always running into things. Melissa says that Missy, the gerbil that died, could steer the ball. She never crashed into anything.

Gerbils can run and leap really far. The more room they have, the happier they are. They burrow, groom themselves, and play. Sometimes they raise up on their hind legs and stand very still. They are listening, on the alert for any sign of danger. Most of the time, of course, there is no danger.

Melissa says gerbils love to play in paper towel tubes. She also gives her gerbils paper towels and tissues to shred. It doesn't take them long to shred up a paper towel.

Melissa and her brother, Michael, and her little sister, Jessica, like to take the gerbils out of the cages. Sometimes Melissa and her friends sit with their legs spread out and touching, so they form a closed circle. The gerbils can't get out of the circle. Melissa and her friends also set up mazes of boxes for the gerbils to crawl through.

When the gerbils run inside the circle, it's like a game. You'd think they'd jump over your legs, but they don't. They just run and explore.

Fun Facts about Gerbils

- Unlike hamsters, gerbils have excellent vision.

- Most pet gerbils are Mongolian gerbils, discovered by a French scientist in the early 1950s. Gerbils came to the United States in 1954.

- The scientific name of the Mongolian gerbil is *Meriones unguiculatus.* Meriones was a warrior in Greek myths. He wore a helmet decorated with the tusks of a wild boar. *Unguiculatus* means "with fingernails or claws" in Latin.

- Half of a gerbil's length is in its tail.

- Gerbils can leap as far as 1½ feet.

- Gerbils have a very good sense of hearing. They can hear low-frequency sounds that humans can't hear.

- When female gerbils give birth, they stand on their back legs and reach down to pull the babies out.

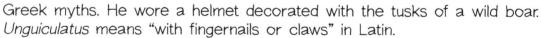

Taming a gerbil is a lot like taming a hamster. It takes a little while. You start by offering it food from your hand. The gerbil will learn to eat from your hand, and it will get used to being touched. Pretty soon it will be running all over you. Gerbils like to climb up your pant legs or your sleeves.

Frisky likes to climb into Melissa's overall pocket. Melissa is good at taming gerbils—she even tamed Sourpuss.

Melissa's family hasn't had any problems with their gerbils, except one time. Jessica loves the gerbils so much that one night she took Frisky to bed with her. In the middle of the night, the gerbil bit her and Jessica was bleeding and crying. Her mom came into her bedroom and saw the blood and wondered what was going on! It looked worse than it was. Jessica wasn't hurt very badly.

I like Melissa's gerbils a lot. Maybe someday I'll get gerbils, too.

Once gerbils start to trust you, they'll mostly behave themselves. A little food always helps.

Lightning is a great pet...

Hamsters don't live to be very old. They have a life span of two or three years. Gerbils live a little bit longer, usually three or four years. I heard of one hamster that lived to be five years old. That's probably like a person who's 110!

Most of the time hamsters and gerbils stay healthy. You don't have to worry about them getting sick. If you spend a lot of time with your pet, you will notice any changes in the way it looks or acts. You'll be able to tell if something is wrong.

Lightning is already over two years old.

Healthy hamsters and gerbils are active and alert. Their eyes are clear and bright, and their fur is smooth and glossy. If their fur is wet near their tail, it could mean they have diarrhea. Gross! Hamsters can also get a disease called "wet tail." They have diarrhea and lose their appetite. It's a serious problem. The hamster usually dies from it.

You will know your hamster or gerbil is sick if it just lies around all the time. It's also sick if it doesn't want to eat. If that happens, you should take your pet to a veterinarian.

Lightning seems like a healthy hamster. So far, she's never been sick.

Hamster Health

Healthy hamsters and gerbils have bright, shiny eyes, a thick, silky coat, a clean tail and rear end, and a dry nose. The animal is lively and alert.

Factors that can lead to illness in hamsters and gerbils include:

- poor-quality food
- lack of a varied diet
- a cage that is in a drafty place or in direct sunlight
- abrupt changes in temperature
- too much or too little humidity

- damp bedding
- lack of opportunities for gnawing, climbing, and burrowing
- keeping several hamsters together
- disruptions while sleeping

Signs that your hamster or gerbil is sick:

- lack of energy
- bald spots
- weight loss
- runny stools (poops)
- dirty, wet fur around tail
- sneezing or rasping
- runny nose
- loss of appetite

- overgrown teeth
- overgrown claws
- avoidance of light
- scratching more than usual
- swollen, red patches of skin
- red or runny eyes
- swollen cheeks

As soon as you notice any sign of illness, take your pet to a vet.

I asked the vet we take Scooter to if we should bring Lightning in for a checkup. Lori, our vet, said that when you first get a hamster or gerbil, it's a good idea to have the animal checked. The vet can make sure it doesn't have parasites, like worms. A lot of people don't even realize that you can take hamsters and gerbils to a vet. But more and more people are doing it.

I think the happier your hamster is, the healthier it will be.

A hamster like Lightning is fun for everyone.

As a hamster or gerbil gets older, it will sleep a lot. It may get up only to eat or to walk around a little. Older hamsters lose weight and they may walk on shaky legs, kind of like old people do.

So far, Lightning hasn't shown any signs of slowing down. She has turned out to be a great pet for me—and for my class.

Glossary

Burrow: to dig and to live in holes and tunnels. Wild hamsters burrow in sand.

Desert: an area of land that cannot support most life because it is too hot and dry. In the wild, hamsters live in deserts.

Diarrhea (dye-uh-*ree*-uh): a condition in which an animal has runny stools (poops). Diarrhea is a sign of an unhealthy diet or an illness.

Humid (*hyoo*-mid): moist. Humid air contains a lot of water.

Instinct (*in*-stinkt): a way of feeling or acting that is natural to an animal, rather than learned

Neuter (*noo*-ter): to remove the sex organs (testicles) from a male animal so that it is unable to reproduce

Omnivorous (ahm-*nih*-vuh-russ): feeding on both plants and animals

Rodent (*rho*-dunt): a small animal with large, sharp teeth that it uses for gnawing

Spay: to remove the sex organs (uterus and ovaries) from a female animal so that it is unable to reproduce

Territory (*ter*-uh-tor-ee): an area chosen by an animal as its own

Resources

American Rat, Mouse & Hamster Society
Roxanne Fitzgerald, President
210 LaVerne
Long Beach, CA 90803
(310) 439-2002
Assists schools in creating rodent displays for
classrooms; provides speakers to youth groups and
animal groups; sponsors competitions; keeps video and
research library.

Delta Society
P. O. Box 1080
Renton, WA 98057
(206) 226-7357
An international organization for studying human-
animal relationships. Will send a list of books on
animal topics.

Humane Society of the U.S.
2100 L Street NW
Washington, DC 20037
Free tips on caring for birds, dogs, cats, and small
mammals.

Tree House Animal Foundation
(312) 784-5488
Specializes in behavior questions. Caller pays long-
distance charges, but consultation is free.

For Further Reading

Arnold, Caroline. *Watching Desert Wildlife.* Minneapolis: Carolrhoda, 1994.

Evans, Mark. *Hamster.* Foreword by Roger Caras. New York: Dorling Kindersley, 1993.

Fischer-Nagel, Heiderose and Andreas. *Inside the Burrow: The Life of the Golden Hamster.* Minneapolis: Carolrhoda, 1986.

Fischer-Nagel, Heiderose and Andreas. *A Look through the Mouse Hole.* Minneapolis: Carolrhoda, 1989.

Hamsters. Edited and rev. by Dr. G. Edgar Folk, Jr., Dept. of Physiology, College of Medicine, State University of Iowa. Neptune City, NJ: T.F.H. Publications, 1990.

Piers, Helen. *Taking Care of Your Pet Gerbil: A Young Pet Owner's Guide.* Hauppage, NY: Barron's, 1993.

Piers, Helen. *Taking Care of Your Pet Hamster: A Young Pet Owner's Guide.* Hauppage, NY: Barron's, 1992.

Robinson, David. *Encyclopedia of Gerbils.* Neptune City, NJ: T.F.H. Publications, 1980.

Sproule, Anna and Michael. *Know Your Pet Hamsters.* New York: Bookwright Press, 1988.

Index

ABOUT THE AUTHOR

LeeAnne Engfer is a writer and editor. She graduated from the University of Minnesota with degrees in journalism and French. Her interests include animals, books, cooking, travel, and yoga. She lives in St. Paul, Minnesota, with three cats.

ABOUT THE PHOTOGRAPHER

Andy King is a native of Boulder, Colorado, and a graduate of Colorado State University. Andy has traveled around the world as a documentary and corporate photographer, and he has worked as a photographer at newspapers in Minnesota and Texas. He lives with his wife, Patricia, and their daughter in St. Paul, Minnesota, where he enjoys mountain biking and playing basketball.